INTRODUCTION TO PYTHON PROGRAMMING
BY - ARNAB BANERJEE

DEDICATED TO MY GRAND FATHER LATE DR. J.N. RAY
AND MY FRIEND MR. GREG ROBERTS

TABLE OF CONTENTS

CHAPTER -1
INTRODUCTION

WHAT IS PYTHON?

Python is a very popular and widely used high level programming language. It was designed by Guido van Rossum and developed by Python Software Foundation back in 1991, it is mainly popular for it's simple syntaxes and easy to write options, I mean you can write a python code in very few lines compared to other languages, so if you can learn how to this, then it will be very much helpful for you.

APPLICATIONS OF PYTHON

There are various applications of python, from compiling simple computer program to designing graphical user interfaces and games, python has a very wide range of applications, so this the language you really should learn.

WHO CAN READ THIS BOOK?

If you are new to python programming or even not started any kind of programming with python then you really should check out this book which should help you and if you are interested to know how to design GUIs (Graphical user interfaces) with python then also you can go through this book.

WHO CAN AVOID THIS BOOK?

If you are already a pro in python and you are looking for some advanced staffs, then you can avoid this book because I will start from very basic, to give priority to the beginners.

WHAT DO YOU NEED TO RUN A PYTHON CODE?

1) I am going to compile all of my python codes with python3, so you should go ahead and download this from https://www.python.org/ and go to the download section and download the latest version (which is probably python 3.4.1 or python 3.4.2) and install that.

2) The next thing you need is Pycharm, which will work as an editor and the compiler you installed will help you to run the code. You can get Pycharm from https://www.jetbrains.com/pycharm/download/ here, you can download the professional edition and try out 30 days free trial, and you also can download this professional edition from torrent.

GOOD TO GO

So we have installed all the necessary software to run a python code and now we are ready to write our first python code. So in the next chapter I will show how you write **your first code.**

CHAPTER -2
YOUR FIRST CODE

PRINTING OUT YOUR FIRST STATEMENT

Now, I will show how you print out a statement using python, and trust me it is the easiest code that you can't even imagine let me show you, how to print a statement using python.

Image 2.1 Printing Hello world

so you can see how easy it is, you just write the print statement and inside that print statement, you have to just type the string(a bunch of words) you want to print out, but make sure that you have typed the string inside of an open a closed speech marks(" <string>").

GIVING AN INPUT:

Now, I will show you how you can give an input to your program, say you want to print out your age and instead of printing it directly you can print it out by giving an input.

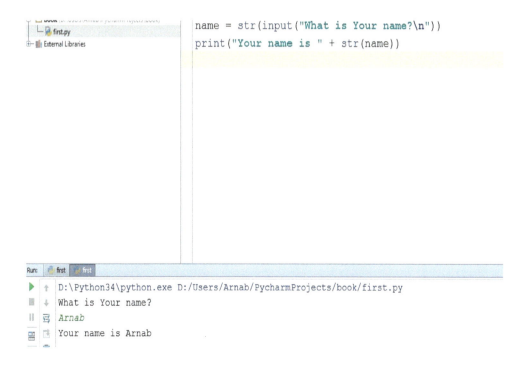

```
age = int(input("What is Your age?\n"))
print("Your age is" + str(age))
```

```
Run:    first    first
    D:\Python34\python.exe D:/Users/Arnab/PycharmProjects/book/first.py
    What is Your age?
    20
    Your age is20
```

Image 2.2 - Giving an integer as input

Code Explanations:

As you can see that I have used a variable named **'age'** which stores the value that user enters, and the keyword **int** allows user to enter an integer value and the keyword **input** allows you to enter the input, and the string that I have used inside **input** prompts to user and asks the user to enter the input.

Now I will show you to how to enter a string as input

```
name = str(input("What is Your name?\n"))
print("Your name is " + str(name))
```

```
Run:    first    first
    D:\Python34\python.exe D:/Users/Arnab/PycharmProjects/book/first.py
    What is Your name?
    Arnab
    Your name is Arnab
```

<u>Image 2.3 – Giving a string as input</u>

As you can see in the above code I have used the keyword **str,** and that allows you to enter a string as a input, so when you are about to enter a integer or number as input use keyword **int** and when you want to enter a string as input use the keyword **str**.

TOWARDS NEXT CHAPTER

In this chapter I have showed you how you can print out any statement using python and also how you can give any kind of input using python, so practice this out, and in the next chapter we will talk about numbers and **arithmetic operations**.

CHAPTER 3
ARITHMATIC OPERATIONS

BASIC IDEA ABOUT OPERATORS AND OPERANDS

Before, you start any kind of arithmetic operations you need to have some idea on what is an operator and what is an operand. So in case you don't know what they are I am explaining it to you in brief. Say, you want to add two numbers say A and B, and you write that expression as (A +B), here the (+) sign works as an operator and A and B are operands, as the (+) sign works on A and B. So on which operators do work are called operands.

SIMPLE ARITHMATIC OPERATIONS:

Now, I will show some simple arithmetic operations like addition, subtraction, multiplication and division using python.

```
book (D:\Users\Arnab\PycharmProjects\book)
    first.py
External Libraries

a = (7+5)
b = (7-5)
c = (7*5)
d = (7/5)
print("The addition result is " + str(a))
print("The subtraction result is " +str(b))
print("The multiplications result is " +str(c))
print("The division result is " +str(d))
```

```
Run:    first    first
    D:\Python34\python.exe D:/Users/Arnab/PycharmProjects/book/first.py
    The addition result is 12
    The subtraction result is 2
    The multiplications result is 35
    The division result is 1.4

    Process finished with exit code 0
```
Image 3.1 - Simple Arithmetic operations

LITTLE BIT COMPLEX ARITHMETICAL OPERATIONS

As I have shown you some basic arithmetical operations, now you should have an idea how it works in python, so now I will show little bit complex staffs, and how python follows the **order of operations.**

```
book (D:\Users\Arnab\PycharmProjects\book)
  first.py
External Libraries
```

```python
a = (9+6*3)
b = ((9+6)*3)
print("The first result is " +str(a))
print("The second result is "+str(b))
```

```
Run:    first   first
    D:\Python34\python.exe D:/Users/Arnab/PycharmProjects/book/first.py
    The first result is 27
    The second result is 45

    Process finished with exit code 0
```

Image 3.2 - Order of operations with python

Explanations

as according to arithmetic mathematics , the order of operations rule states that the multiplication task must be done before addition, and you can see that result when I printed out the value of **'a'** in image 3.2, where the multiplication task is performed before the addition task, but when you close any operations with parenthesis , that operation must be performed first, and you can see that result when I printed the value of **'b'** , where the addition task is performed first when it is closed by parenthesis, and after that the multiplication task is performed.

How to get the round up and remainder during division?

While performing the basic arithmetic operation the result we got during division operation was a fraction value (Image 3.1), so what if we want to get only that integer value and no fraction value or only the remainder value, now I will show how to do this.

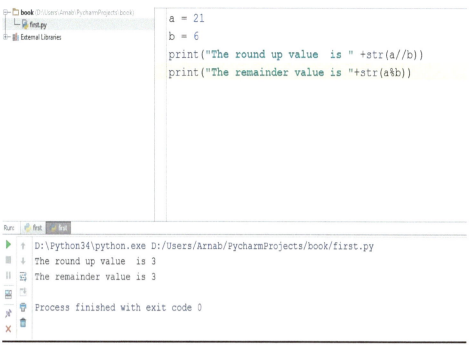

```
a = 21
b = 6
print("The round up value  is " +str(a//b))
print("The remainder value is "+str(a%b))
```

```
Run:    first    first
    D:\Python34\python.exe D:/Users/Arnab/PycharmProjects/book/first.py
    The round up value  is 3
    The remainder value is 3

    Process finished with exit code 0
```

Image 3.3 - how to get round up and remainder

so, when you want to have the round up figure while operating the division of two numbers you need to have (//) operators, and when you need the remainder you need to have (%) operator.

THE 'To-The-Power' OPERATION

Now, I will show you how you can implement a **'to the power'** operation using python. Say, you want to get the result of the operation m 'to the power n' and to get that you have to use the operator (* *), so to get the result you have to write (m ** n), I am giving you an example.

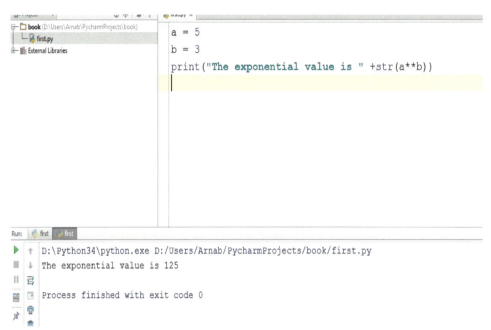

```
a = 5
b = 3
print("The exponential value is " +str(a**b))
```

```
D:\Python34\python.exe D:/Users/Arnab/PycharmProjects/book/first.py
The exponential value is 125

Process finished with exit code 0
```

Image 3.4 –Implementing 'to-the power' function

Move On

so, we have learned about some cool arithmetic operations in this chapter, hopefully you got the basic idea about how this operations work, and you really should practice these things out, and in the next chapter I will talk about **lists**.

CHAPTER -4
LISTS

What is list?
A list in python can be defined as a set of variables or strings. And to declare a list you must use square parenthesis and inside that parenthesis, you can store the items of your list. Let me give an example.

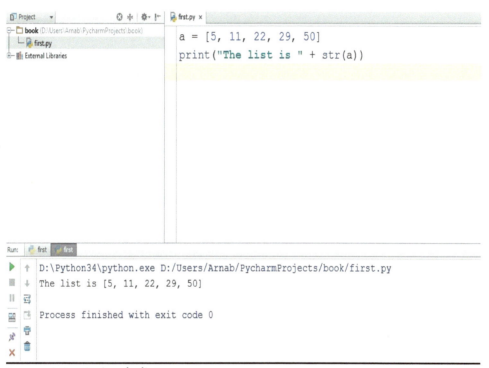

Image 4.1 – A simple list

ADDITION OF TWO LISTS
Now, I will show, how to add two lists, when you are doing an addition of two list the result will contain all the items of the two lists.

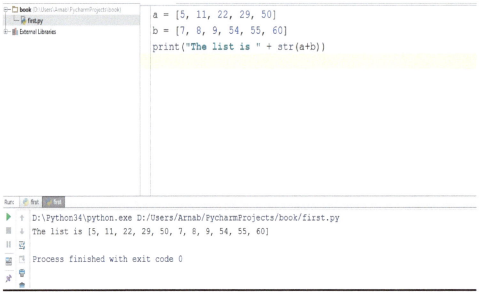

```
a = [5, 11, 22, 29, 50]
b = [7, 8, 9, 54, 55, 60]
print("The list is " + str(a+b))
```

```
Run:    first    first
    D:\Python34\python.exe D:/Users/Arnab/PycharmProjects/book/first.py
    The list is [5, 11, 22, 29, 50, 7, 8, 9, 54, 55, 60]

    Process finished with exit code 0
```

Image 4.2 – Addition of two lists

so, in image 4.2 you can see that the addition result contains all the items in both of the lists.

ADD ITEMS TO A PARTICULAR LIST

I have shown you how to add two lists, but it does not change the value of any of the lists separately, so now I will show you how to add items to particular list and change the value of that list.

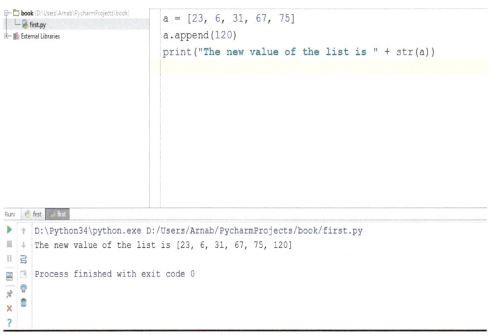

```
a = [23, 6, 31, 67, 75]
a.append(120)
print("The new value of the list is " + str(a))
```

```
Run:    first    first
    D:\Python34\python.exe D:/Users/Arnab/PycharmProjects/book/first.py
    The new value of the list is [23, 6, 31, 67, 75, 120]

    Process finished with exit code 0
```

Image 4.3 – How to add items to a list

Explanations

now, you can see (in image 4.3) the list 'a' which is consist of items like [23, 6, 31, 67, 75] and I wanted to add another item in that list say, 120 and it will change the value of the list permanently (until and unless I delete that item from that list), so to do that I have used a keyword **'append'**, so keep that in mind when you want to add items to a particular list permanently use **the list name. append,** here the name of the list is 'a', hence I have used **a. append.**

SEARCH ANY ITEM IN THE LIST:

Now, if you want to search any element/item , you can do it very easily, say if you want to search the second element in the list, you have to just print out the value of **'a[2]',** since computer starts counting from 0. Just like the value of **'a[0]'** will be the first element in the list. Let me show you an example.

```
a = [23, 6, 31, 67, 75]
print("The searched element of the list is  " + str(a[2]))
```

```
D:\Python34\python.exe D:/Users/Arnab/PycharmProjects/book/first.py
The searched element of the list is  31

Process finished with exit code 0
```

Image 4.4 – Searching an element in the list

as, you can see in the image 4.4, I wanted to search the third item in the list and hence I have printed out the value of **'a[2]',** now you should be able to search any element in the list.

PRINTING THE VALUE UP TO CERTAIN RANGE:

Say, you have a list of 10 items in it, but you want to get only first five elements of that list or the last five elements of the list or the middle elements, So in this example I am going to show you how you can do it and after that I will explain it to you.

```
a = [23, 6, 31, 67, 75, 88, 69, 29, 22, 50]
print("The first five elements of the list are  " + str(a[:5]))
print("The second five elements of the list are  " + str(a[5:]))
print("The middle elements of the list are " + str(a[2:7]))
```

```
D:\Python34\python.exe D:/Users/Arnab/PycharmProjects/book/first.py
The first five elements of the list are  [23, 6, 31, 67, 75]
The second five elements of the list are  [88, 69, 29, 22, 50]
The middle elements of the list are [31, 67, 75, 88, 69]

Process finished with exit code 0
```

Image 4.5 Range in lists

Explanations:

I am starting my explanations from printing out middle range elements, as you can see in the example (Image 4.5) I have printed out the value of **'a[2:7]'** and that means I wanted the range of 3rd element to 8th element of that list, so when you want any range first use the (:) sign, and to the right side of that side is from which element I want to start and to the left side is at which element I want to stop.

Now you can see where I printed the first five elements I have used nothing in the right side of that (:) sign and that basically means start from the first element and stop at 5th element.

And look at where I printed out the last 5 elements, in that case I have used (-5) to the right side of (:) and that means start from the 5th last element and stop at extreme last element (as the left side of (:) is kept blank).

Delete Any element from the list:

Now, if you think that you got some un-necessary elements in your list and you want to delete them, I am showing you how you can do it real quick, first look at the example.

```
book (D:\Users\Arnab\PycharmProjects\book)
  first.py
External Libraries
```

```
a = [23, 6, 31, 67, 75, 88, 69]
a[:3] = []
print("The depleted list is " + str(a))
```

```
Run:    first    first
    D:\Python34\python.exe D:/Users/Arnab/PycharmProjects/book/first.py
    The depleted list is [67, 75, 88, 69]

    Process finished with exit code 0
```

Image 4.6 Delete elements from a list

Explanations:

Now in the above example (Image 4.6) I wanted to delete the first 3 elements of the list, so you can see I have replaced the value of those elements with null value(using open and close square brackets), and it basically delete those elements from the list. Similarly if you want to change the value of any item of the list you can do it using this technique , say if you want to replace the value of 3rd item of the list with 38, just type **'a[2]'** = 38, and your value will be replaced.

USING STRINGS IN LISTS:

In the previous examples I have used numbers in the list but similarly strings can be used in the list, but basically all the properties of list do not change while strings are used but still I am showing you an example where strings are used in a list.

```
months = ['jan', 'feb', 'mar', 'apr', 'may', 'jun', 'jul', 'aug', 'sep', 'oct']

print("The 6th month is " + str(months[5]))
```

```
D:\Python34\python.exe D:/Users/Arnab/PycharmProjects/book/first.py
The 6th month is jun

Process finished with exit code 0
```

Image 4.7 – Using strings in lists

STORE LISTS IN A LIST

Like strings and numbers, lists also can be stored in a list, and it is very
handy application of list,

you can store as many list as you like in list, and those lists can be of
different data types as well.

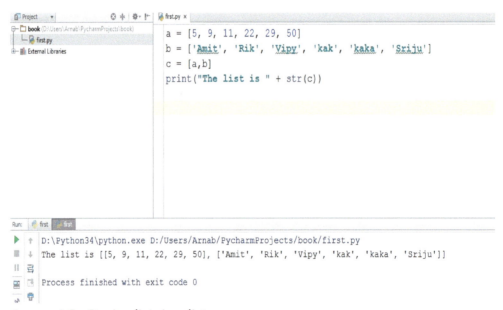

```
a = [5, 9, 11, 22, 29, 50]
b = ['Amit', 'Rik', 'Vipy', 'kak', 'kaka', 'Sriju']
c = [a,b]
print("The list is " + str(c))
```

```
D:\Python34\python.exe D:/Users/Arnab/PycharmProjects/book/first.py
The list is [[5, 9, 11, 22, 29, 50], ['Amit', 'Rik', 'Vipy', 'kak', 'kaka', 'Sriju']]

Process finished with exit code 0
```

Image 4.8 - Storing lists in a list

In Image 4.8 you can see that I have stored two lists in a new list 'c', and
both of lists 'a' and 'b' are of different data types. So this should be clear
to you. And you should be able to store items in a list.

TOWARDS NEXT CHAPTER:

So, in this chapter we have learned about various properties of lists, just practice these things and now we are good enough to move on towards our next chapter where I will talk about various **operators**.

CHAPTER 5
OPERATORS

WHAT IS AN OPERATOR?
Operator is a symbol that allows performing any kind of programming operations, there are various kinds of operators in programming. Now, I will discuss about all kind of operators that are used in python.

CLASSIFICATION OF OPERATORS:
Operators can be classified into various types like wise
1) Arithmetic Operators.
2) Bit-wise Operators.
3) Logical Operators
4) Relational Operators or Comparison Operators
5) Assignment Operators
6) Membership Operators
7) Identity Operators

ARITHMETIC OPERATORS:
I have discussed about most part of the arithmetic operators in the **Chapter - 3(ARITHMATIC OPERATIONS)** of this book, so you really want to check that out.

BIT-WISE OPERATORS:
Bitwise operators in python are such operators that perform bit by bit operations, I will illustrate it to you by an example, and then I will explain it to you.

```
book (D:\Users\Arnab\PycharmProjects\book)
  first.py
  External Libraries
```

```python
a = 15
b = 10
print("The binary form of a is " + bin(a))
print("The binary form of b is " + bin(b))
print("The 'AND' operation result is " + bin(a & b))
```

```
Run:    first    first

  D:\Python34\python.exe D:/Users/Arnab/PycharmProjects/book/first.py
  The binary form of a is 0b1111
  The binary form of b is 0b1010
  The 'AND' operation result is 0b1010

  Process finished with exit code 0
```

Image 5.1 Bitwise operators (AND operation)

Explanations:

According to image 5.1 I have assumed two numbers **'a = 15'** and **'b=10'** , now first you can see that I have converted **'a'** to its equivalent binary number(The keyword **'bin'** converts a number to its equivalent binary number) which is **1111** as you can see, and I have done the same thing for **'b'**, and in this case the equivalent binary number is **1010**. And after that I have performed a bit by bit **and** operations of those numbers, I mean the **and** operation between (**1111** & **1010**), hence the result is **1010** as you can see.
[Starting from **right most digits** of two binary numbers, the result of **and** operation is (1&0 =0, 1&1 =1, 1&0 =0, 1&1 =1]. Hence the result is **1010**. And the symbol **'&'** is a **bitwise AND operator**.

REMEMBER: **1** means a **true value** and **0** means a **false value**.

Other bitwise operations and explanations:

Now, I will show other bitwise operations like **'or'** and **'ex-or'** operations, and then I will explain the operations.

OR –OPERATION:

```
book [D:\Users\Arnab\PycharmProjects\book]          a = 15
    first.py                                        b = 10
External Libraries                                  print("The binary form of a is " + bin(a))
                                                    print("The binary form of b is " + bin(b))
                                                    print("The 'AND' operation result is " + bin(a | b))
```

```
Run:    first    first
    D:\Python34\python.exe D:/Users/Arnab/PycharmProjects/book/first.py
    The binary form of a is 0b1111
    The binary form of b is 0b1010
    The 'AND' operation result is 0b1111

    Process finished with exit code 0
```

Image 5.2 Bitwise operators (Or operation)

Explanations:

According to image 5.2` similarly like previous example I have assumed tow numbers **'a= 15'** and **'b=10'**, and then I have converted them to their equivalent binary digits which are **1111** and **1010** respectively. And then I have performed the 'OR' operation between them, and the symbol **'|'** is a **bitwise OR operator.** [Starting from the **right most digits** of two binary numbers, the result of the **OR** operation is (1 | 0 =1, 1 | 1 =1, 1 | 0 =1, 1 | 1 =1) Hence the result of the **OR** operation is **1111**.

REMEMBER: **1** means a **true value** and **0** means a **false value.**

EX-OR OPERATION:

```
book (D:\Users\Arnab\PycharmProjects\book)
    first.py
External Libraries

a = 15
b = 10
print("The binary form of a is " + bin(a))
print("The binary form of b is " + bin(b))
print("The 'AND' operation result is " + bin(a ^ b))
```

```
Run:    first    first
    D:\Python34\python.exe D:/Users/Arnab/PycharmProjects/book/first.py
    The binary form of a is 0b1111
    The binary form of b is 0b1010
    The 'AND' operation result is 0b101

    Process finished with exit code 0
```

Image 5.3 - Bitwise Ex-Or Operator

Explanations:

And you can see like previous two example I took that same two numbers but this time I have performed an Ex-Or operation. And the symbol '^' is a **bit wise EX-OR operator**.

[Starting from the right most digits of two numbers, the result of the EX-OR operation is (1 ^ 0 =1, 1 ^ 1 =0, 1^0 =1, 1 ^ 1 =0), Hence the result is **101**, you can see the left most **0** is ignored just because it has no effects on the original binary number.

REMEMBER: **1** means a **true value** and **0** means a **false value.**

LOGICAL OPERATORS:

Logical operators works on **macro level true or false values** while bitwise operators operates on bit by bit values a logical operator works on the total value. Let me give you an example.

```
book (D:\Users\Arnab\PycharmProjects\book)
    first.py
External Libraries

a = True
b = False
c = True
d = False
print("1st logical 'AND' operation result is " + str(a and b))
print("2nd logical 'AND operation result is " + str(a and c))
print("1st logical 'OR' operation result is " + str(a or b))
print("2nd logical 'OR' operation result is " + str(b or d))
print("1st logical 'NOT' operation result is " + str(a))
print("2nd logical 'NOT' operation result is " + str(b))
```

```
Run:    first    first
D:\Python34\python.exe D:/Users/Arnab/PycharmProjects/book/first.py
1st logical 'AND' operation result is False
2nd logical 'AND operation result is True
1st logical 'OR' operation result is True
2nd logical 'OR' operation result is False
1st logical 'NOT' operation result is True
2nd logical 'NOT' operation result is False

Process finished with exit code 0
```

Image 5.4 – Logical operators.

Explanations:

I have assumed four variables, which has only Boolean values(True, False), and now I have performed some logical operation like **'and'**, **'or'**, **'not'**. Now you can see, when I have performed the **'logical and'** operation between two variables **'a and b'**, we get the result as **'False'**, and when I have performed the **'logical and'** operation between two variables **'a and c'** we get the result as a' **True'** value(So a logical and operation between **one True value and one False value** is always results a **False value** and a logical operation between **two True value always results a True value**, similarly a logical and operation between **two False value always results a False value.**).

Next I have performed the **'Logical or'** operation, and for a **'logical or'** operation if one variable is **True**, and one is false the operation will result a **True value**, if both of the variables are **True**, then also the operation will result a **True value**, but if both of the variables are **False**, then the operation will result a **False value**.

And a **'Logical NOT'** operation just inverts the value, as you can see in the example, the value of **'a'** was **True**, but after performing the **Not** operation the result is **False**.

RELATIONAL OR COMPARISON OPERATORS:

Relational or comparison operators are those operators, which helps us to relate or compare between two variables, this operators are used for two variables to check if they are **equal to(==)**, **non-equal to(!=)**, **greater than(>)** or **less than(<)** to each other. I am showing you what a relational operator is with the help of an **if-else** statement and later I will explain what an **if-else** statement is, so don't be worry about it.

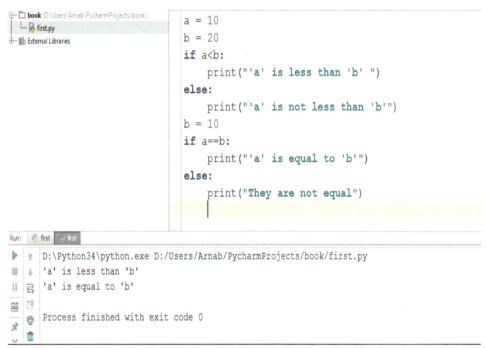

```
book (D:\Users\Arnab\PycharmProjects\book)
    first.py
External Libraries

a = 10
b = 20
if a<b:
    print ("'a' is less than 'b' ")
else:
    print ("'a' is not less than 'b'")
b = 10
if a==b:
    print ("'a' is equal to 'b'")
else:
    print ("They are not equal")
```

```
Run:    first    first

D:\Python34\python.exe D:/Users/Arnab/PycharmProjects/book/first.py
'a' is less than 'b'
'a' is equal to 'b'

Process finished with exit code 0
```

Image 5.5 – Relational operators

Explanations:
say, I have assumed couple of variables, **'a =10'** and **'b =20'**, now with the if-statement I simply checked if the value of **'a'** is less than **'b'** or not, and this program simply means if the value is less than **'b'** then simply **print out the statement which is under 'if' statement**, if it is not then **print out the statement which is under 'else' statement.**
Next I have set the value of variable **'b =10'**, so now **a = b** and the (==) sign in that **'if'** statement simply checks if those value are equal to each other or not, if they are equal to each other, then print out the statement under 'if' statement otherwise printout out the statement which is under that 'else' statement.
Hence the symbols like (==), (! =), (<), (>), (<=), (>=) are all relational operators.

MEMBERSHIP OPERATOR:

Now, Membership operators are such operators that helps you to check if a certain string or number is present in a particular set of string or number, or not. Let me show you an example of membership operators, but before that I want to mention that the keyword **'in'** do work as a membership operator. So now look at the example.

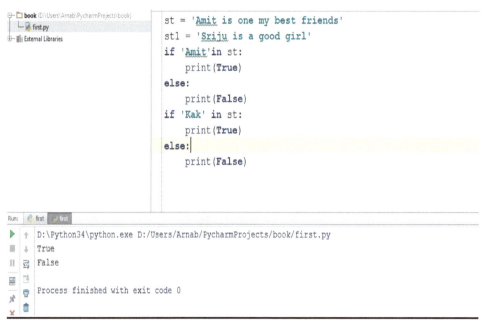

Image 5.6 –Membership operators

Explanations:

As you can see in image 5.6, I took couple of string variables **'st'** and **'st1'**, and next in the first 'if' statement I checked if a particular string is present in that set of string or not, since it was present, it printed out the value **'True'**, and next I checked for the second set of string **'st1'**, and checked if a certain string is present in that set of string or not and science it was not present it printed out the value under the **'else'** statement.

IDENTITY OPERATORS:

Identity operators allows us to check if the two variable are identical or not, I mean if they have same values and data types or not. Let me explain it with an example. And the keyword **'is'** works as an identity operator.

```
book (D:\Users\Arnab\PycharmProjects\book)          a = 20
    first.py                                        b = '20'
External Libraries                                  if a is b:
                                                        print(True)
                                                    else:
                                                        print(False)
                                                    b = 20
                                                    if a is b:
                                                        print(True)
                                                    else:
                                                        print(False)

Run:    first    first
        D:\Python34\python.exe D:/Users/Arnab/PycharmProjects/book/first.py
        False
        True

        Process finished with exit code 0
```

Image 5.6 – Identity operators

Explanations:

Look at the example(Image 5.6) very carefully, I took two variables, **'a'** and **'b'** and both are of same value but are of different data types one is an integer and another one is a string, and since they are not of same value and data type, it printed the value which is under **else statement, which is False**.

Next I have changed the data type of **'b'** from string to integer and since both the variables 'a' and 'b' are of similar value and data type, **it printed the value True.**

ASSIGNMENT OPERATORS AND DIFFERENCE BETWEEN (=) AND (==) SIGN:

Now, I will talk about something which is little bit conceptual, I will talk about assignment operator, and generally the symbol **'='** is used as an assignment operator.

Now, you guys probably wondering what is the difference between **('=')** and **('= = ')** sign.

Well, (==) sign is basically a relational operator, I mean if value of both variables say, **'a'** and **'b'** are same, then by this symbol you can say that they are equal to each other.

But, say the value of **'a'** is **20** and you want to assign this value to another variable, say **'b'**, so to assign this value you have to write **'a = b'** and this is called an **assignment operation** and **'=' symbol is an assignment operator**.

TOWARDS NEXT CHAPTER:

So, that is all what I got for operators, hopefully it is now crystal clear to you, just try and practice these codes, play around with it, and in the next chapter we will discuss about **if, el-if and else statements.**

CHAPTER -6
If, el-if, and else statements

WHAT IS AN IF SATEMENT?

An if statement generally used for making a decision, but with the help of a simple if statement only on decision can be made, just look at the example how it happens.

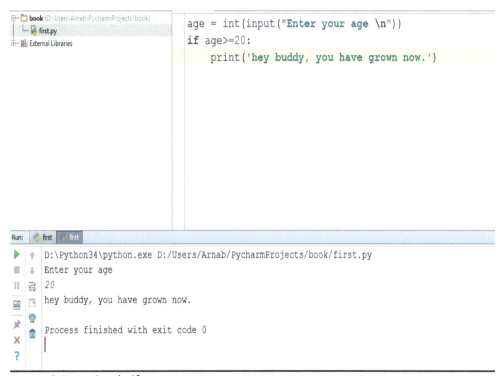

Image 6.1 – a simple if statement

Explanations:

Here(according to image 6.1) I have made an simple if statement which asks to enter my age, and if my age is greater than or equal to 20, then it will print out the statement under the if statement, if it less than 20, then it will print out nothing, and this the limitations of simple if statement.

NOTE: Please note that when you are making an **'if'** or **'if- else'** statement make sure that **you write them in a correct indented form**, otherwise you will get an **indentation block error**. So please be very **careful** about it.

WHAT IS AN IF-ELSE STATEMENT?

Now, an 'if-else' statement is kind of extension of a simple 'if' statement, it generally means the if the condition is not satisfied under 'if' statement, perform the task which is under else statement, Let me show you an example.

```
age = int(input("Enter your age \n"))
if age<=20:
    print('You are quite young to work')
elif 21 <= age <= 60:
    print("You should be fit to work")
else:
    print("You are getting old for work!!")
```

```
book (D:\Users\Arnab\PycharmProjects\book)
    first.py
External Libraries
```

```
Run:    first    first    first
    D:\Python34\python.exe D:/Users/Arnab/PycharmProjects/book/first.py
    Enter your age
    54
    You should be fit to work

    Process finished with exit code 0
```

Image 6.2 – an if-else statement.

Explanations:
Now, according to Image 6.2, there is an 'if-else' statement which checks your age, and if the age is greater than or equal to 20, it prints a certain string, and if it is not (less than 20) it prints out a different string.
Since, I have entered age as 19, hence it has printed out the value under else statement, as 19 is not greater than or equal to 20.
So practice these codes with correct indentations and it be clear to you.

And, now I will move on little bit complex 'if-else' statements, which is 'if-el-if-else' statements.

WHAT IS AN 'if-elif-else' STATEMENT?
In simple words it is more applicable for making more than two decisions, as and 'if-else' statement check couple of conditions but when more than two conditions is to be checked, then this statement comes into play.
Look at the example.

```
age = int(input("Enter your age \n"))
if age<=20:
    print('You are quite young to work')
    weight = int(input("Enter your body weight in pounds\n"))
    if weight>180:
        print("You need to go to gym!")
    else:
        print("You are ok, you don't need gym now!")
elif 60 >= age >= 21:
    print("You should be fit to work")
else:
    print("You are getting old for work!!")
```

```
Runs    first    first    first

D:\Python34\python.exe D:/Users/Arnab/PycharmProjects/book/first.py
Enter your age
20
You are quite young to work
Enter your body weight in pounds
140
You are ok, you don't need gym now!

Process finished with exit code 0
```

Image 6.3 – an 'if-elif-else statement

Explanations:

According to image 6.3 the 'if-else' statements also checks the age like previous example, but you can see, the entered age is 54, which neither satisfies the condition of 'if' statement nor the 'else' statement, but it satisfies the condition of 'el-if' statement which lies between the 'if' and 'else' statements. Hence the task under that 'el-if' statement is performed. So you can make as many 'el-if' as you want depending on the number of choices you want to make.

So, hopefully it is now crystal clear to you.

A NESTED if-else STATEMENT:

When you have an 'if-else' statement, inside/under of another 'if' statement or 'else' statement, then it is called nested 'if-else' statement.

```python
age = int(input("Enter your age \n"))
if age<=20:
    print('You are quite young to work')
    weight = int(input("Enter your body weight in pounds\n"))
    if weight>180:
        print("You need to go to gym!")
    else:
        print("You are ok, you don't need gym now!")
elif 60 >= age >= 21:
    print("You should be fit to work")
else:
    print("You are still a kid!!")
```

Run: first   first   first

```
D:\Python34\python.exe D:/Users/Arnab/PycharmProjects/book/first.py
Enter your age
20
You are quite young to work
Enter your body weight in pounds
140
You are ok, you don't need gym now!

Process finished with exit code 0
```

Image 6.4 – A nested 'if-else' statement

Explanations:

If you follow image 6.4 you can see that under the first if statement, I have made a nested 'if-else' statement. After you enter your age and if it is less than 20 then that nested 'if-else' statement will execute, and it will ask for your body weight, and if it is more than 180 it will print out a certain string and if it is less it will print out a different string, and if the entered age is not less than 20, then that nested 'if-else' statement will not execute.

NEXT-DESTINATION:

So, we have learned about most part of 'if-else' statements, just practice theses codes out and make sure you do it with correct indentations, otherwise your code will not execute properly, and in next chapter we will discuss about **loops**.

CHAPTER – 7
LOOPS

WHAT IS A LOOP?

A loop is that arrangement or sequence, that allows the user to loop through bit of code, I mean a loop just repeats to compile the codes under it. And in this chapter, basically I am going to talk about **two types** of loops, **1) for loop 2) while loop.**

1) FOR LOOP:

WHEN WE NEED A FOR LOOP?

So, now the concept of list will come into play little bit, say, we have a list, which consist of 4 items, and if you want to print those items out you can do it with 4 print statements, but what if you got 100 items in a list and then if you want to print them out with just print statements then it's going to take one heck of a time and line of codes, so to deal with this problem, the concept of loop will come into play, and this time I will show it with a **'for loop'**. So just look at the example.

```
book
  first.py
  External Libraries

friends= ['Amit','Kaka', 'Rik','Sriju', 'Roon', 'Soutrick', 'Anie', 'TD']
for a in friends:
    print("Name of friend is " +str(a))
```

```
Run:    first   first   first
  D:\Python34\python.exe D:/Users/Arnab/PycharmProjects/book/first.py
  Name of friend is Amit
  Name of friend is Kaka
  Name of friend is Rik
  Name of friend is Sriju
  Name of friend is Roon
  Name of friend is Soutrick
  Name of friend is Anie
  Name of friend is TD

  Process finished with exit code 0
```

Image 7.1 – A for Loop

Explanations:

Now in the example (Image 7.1) you can see that I have list of friend names, and I wanted to print them out, so instead of doing it one by one I have used a for loop(and the output is same), and in the for loop, I have used a variable name **'a'** and when I wanted to loop through that list, for the first time when the loop compiles **'a'** is basically equals to the first member of that list, and after each time the loop is completed **'a'** is equal to the next member of that list.

So, this is basic of a 'for loop', and like this you can write as many codes as you can. I will show more examples later.

2) WHILE LOOP:

WHEN WE NEED A WHILE LOOP?

Now, what while loop does in python, is they first check a certain condition, and it loops through the codes under it, until and unless that condition is true, when the condition turns out as false, the loop terminates. Let me show an example.

```python
age = int(input("Please enter your age!!\n"))
while age <=60:
    print('You are still efficient to work!')
    age +=1
```

```
D:\Python34\python.exe D:/Users/Arnab/PycharmProjects/book/first.py
Please enter your age!!
55
You are still efficient to work!
You are still efficient to work!
You are still efficient to work!
You are still efficient to work!
You are still efficient to work!
You are still efficient to work!

Process finished with exit code 0
```

Image 7.2 – While loop

Explanations:

Now, according to (Image 7.2), I have entered an age, and the while loop executes if and only if age is less than 50. The age I entered is 45, so the code under while loop executes, and then I have incremented age by one (as the each time the while loop loops through the code, the value of each will be increased by value 1 or the loop will run for infinite number of time and it will never terminate). So you can see after the value of age = 50, the loop terminates. So this is how a while loop works.

CONCEPT OF RANGE:

Say, if you want to print out numbers with in certain range, and you don't have lists, then this concept comes into play, look at the example.

Image 7.1 – RANGE

here, I wanted to print out numbers within range of 0 and 31, and with 5 increment, that means, say the first number is '**x**', then the next number will be '**(x+5)**', and so on.

THIS IS ALL ABOUT BASIC LOOPS:

So, what I have discussed in this chapter, it is all about basic loops, though I will show more application of loops later, so practice these things, and in the net chapter we will talk about **functions and modules.**

CHAPTER 8
FUNCTIONS AND MODULES

WHAT IS A FUNCTION?

Now, so far we have written bunch of lines of codes and have performed some tasks, but we can do those tasks as many times as we want and at any time using functions. I am just showing you a simple example and then I will explain it.

Image 8.1 – A basic function

Explanations:

Now, follow the example(Image 8.1), so the first thing you need to remember when you are creating a function you have to use the keyword **'def'**, and then the name of your function, the name of my function in the example is **'first'**, hence the first line of code is **'def first()'**, and make sure that you use parenthesis right after the name of your function, otherwise your function won't work, and inside this function I have used a print statement, and to print out that statement, I have called/used the function in the 3rd line of the program. **And remember if you don't call/use your function, the codes inside** your function won't come into play and in this case if I did not called that function that string/statement wouldn't be printed out.

USING A FUNCTION WITH ARGUMENTS:

Now, I will show you how you can pass an argument in a function, first look at the example, and then I will explain it to you.

```python
def weight(pound):
    kg = pound/2.2
    print("Your weight in kg is " + str(kg) + " kg")
weight(100)
```

```
D:\Python34\python.exe D:/Users/Arnab/PycharmProjects/book/first.py
Your weight in kg is 45.45454545454545 kg

Process finished with exit code 0
```

Image 8.2 – Passing an argument

Explanations:

So, in the previous example (In image 8.2) I have used a function named 'weight', and passed an argument in it, now first of all what this function does is basically it converts weight(pounds to kilograms), so I wanted to make a function where, if user enters a weight in pounds, the function will print that corresponding weight into kilograms, so to implement that function you can see I have used a formula (**kg = pound / 2.2**), and after that I have printed out the value of weight in kilograms, so you can see when I wanted to convert 100 pounds of weight it gave me the value of 45.45 kg, (look very carefully at the example0), so this is a very basic example of passing an argument in a function.

CONCEPT OF 'RETURN' VALUES:

Now, so far in our functions we have printed out a direct statement or string, and we have learnt how to pass an argument, and make some kind of calculations inside of a function, and then we have printed that out. Well, sometimes we have to do, some kind of calculations inside a function, but unlike previous times instead of printing it out directly we will store that result in a variable, and we will use that result later in that function, and we can manipulate this idea with **'return'** statements. I am showing you an example to make things crystal clear to you.

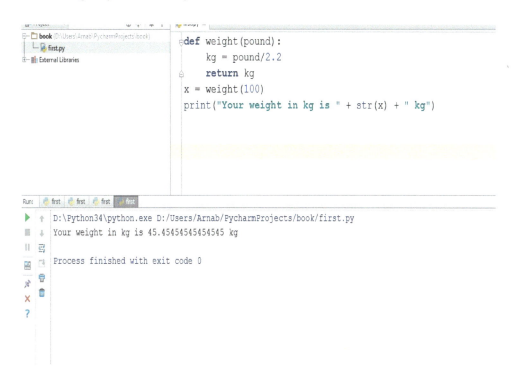

Image 8.3 – A Return statement

Explanations:
Now, If you see the example carefully (Image 8.3) you can see that I have done the same calculation, what I have done in my previous function, but this time I did it with a return statement to make things clear to you. Now what the return statement is doing here is it collects the result value and stores it in a variable called 'x', so when I want to print out 'x', it gives me the corresponding result of the calculation, you really need to practice these things out to get this concept in details.

PASSING A DEFAULT VALUE FOR AN ARGUMENT:

I have showed how to pass an argument in a function in one of the previous examples, but now I will show how to pass a default value as an argument, it is applicable when, say, you are making a calculation like previous examples, but assume that the user haven't passed any value in that function, then that argument will use that default value in the function. Again look at the example very carefully.

```
book (D:\Users\Arnab\PycharmProjects\book)         def weight(pound = 'No value is entered'):
    first.py                                            if weight is 'valid':
External Libraries                                          x = int(input("Please enter the weight \n"))
                                                            kg = x/2.2
                                                            print("Your weight in kg is " + str(kg) + " kg")
                                                        else:
                                                            print(pound)
                                                    weight()
```

```
Run:    first    first    first    first
    D:\Python34\python.exe D:/Users/Arnab/PycharmProjects/book/first.py
    No value is entered

    Process finished with exit code 0
```

Image 8.4- Default value for an argument.

Explanations:

The very first thing you can see in the example(Image 8.4) is that I have used an 'if-else' statement, to manipulate the function, and if user passes any value as argument then the codes under 'if' block will come into play otherwise 'else' block will execute, and when that 'else' block is going to execute, a default value for argument will be used, which is **'no value is entered'** . So this is how a default value for an argument should be passed.

GLOBAL AND LOCAL VARIABLES:

Now, I will talk about global and local variables, and how they are used in different functions. First I will talk about global variables and then local variables, after that you can easily figure out the difference between them.

GLOBAL VARIABLES:

If a variable is declared globally, I mean outside of all the functions that are present in the program, then that variable is called a global variable, please remember that all the function in that program can access that variable. Now let me show an example.

```
age = int(input("Enter your age \n"))
def function1(name):
    print("Your age is " + str(age) + " Your name is " + str(name))
def function2(team):
    print("Your age is " + str(age) + " Your team is " + str(team))
function1('Arnab')
function2('KKR')
```

```
Run:    first    first    first    first
D:\Python34\python.exe D:/Users/Arnab/PycharmProjects/book/first.py
Enter your age
20
Your age is 20 Your name is Arnab
Your age is 20 Your team is KKR

Process finished with exit code 0
```

Image 8.5 -Global variables.

Explanations:

Now, if you have noticed the example carefully, then you can see that I have used a variable named **'age'**, outside both of the functions, **('function1' and 'function2)** which holds the value of age what user gives. Though that variable was not declared inside of any function, but I have used that function successfully inside both of those functions, just because it is a global variable. If that variable was declared inside of a function, then I would not be able to use that variable in both of the functions.

LOCAL VARIABLES*:*

If any variable is declared inside of a function, then this variable can't be used in any other functions, such type of variable is called local variables, this kind of variables is not available globally. Now I am showing you an example of local variables.

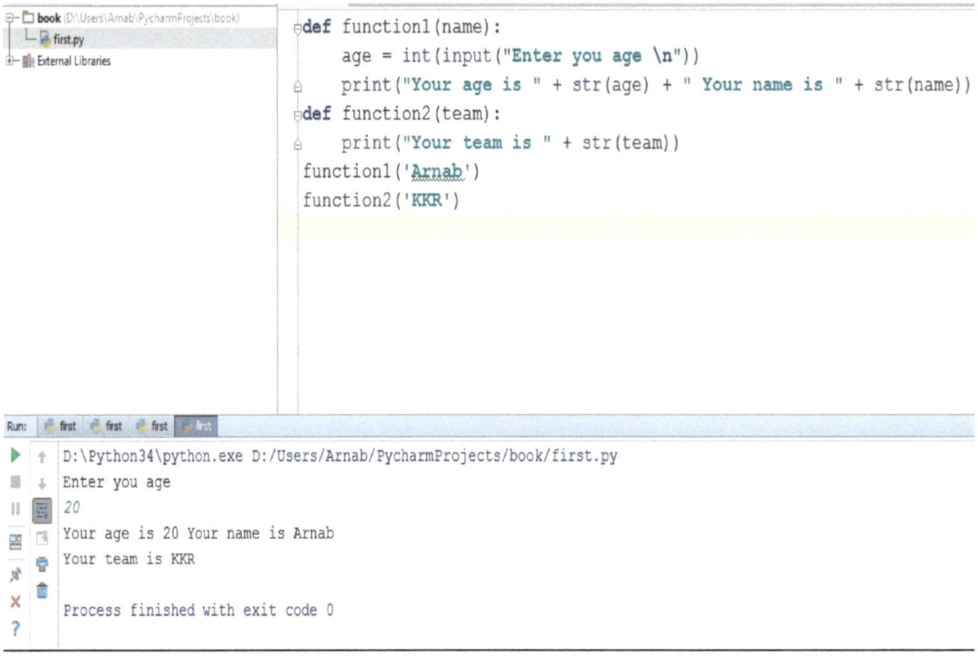

```
def function1(name):
    age = int(input("Enter you age \n"))
    print("Your age is " + str(age) + " Your name is " + str(name))
def function2(team):
    print("Your team is " + str(team))
function1('Arnab')
function2('KKR')
```

```
Run:    first    first    first    first
D:\Python34\python.exe D:/Users/Arnab/PycharmProjects/book/first.py
Enter you age
20
Your age is 20 Your name is Arnab
Your team is KKR

Process finished with exit code 0
```

Image 8.6 – Local variables.

Explanations:

Now, you can see in this example(Image 8.6), I have used that same variable named **'age'**, inside of a function named **'function1'**, so this now a local variable and this variable will not be available for use in the other function which is **'function2'**, just because the variable is declared locally not globally.

MODULES

WHAT IS MODULES?

Just assume that you have made a function that you want to use over and over again, not just in a single program, but in various programs, then you can store that function in a file and it is called modules. Let me show you how you can create a module. I will take two images to explain it to you.

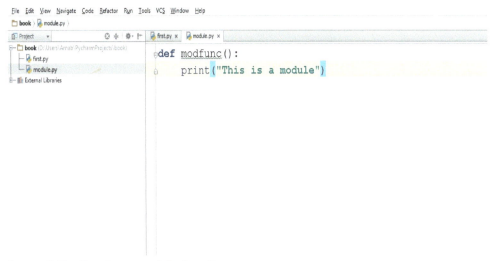

Image 8.7 – Create a module function.

Now, here, I have first created a new file named **'module'**, (**now you can name your file whatever you want**) and in that new file I have created a function named as **'modfunc'**, now next I will show you how you can use this function as a module.

Image 8.8 – Using a function as module.

So, to use a function as module you have to first import that file in your main file, (in this case the name of the file is **'module')**. And to use that function you just can't call that function like you do it in normal time, you have code it like **'file name. function name()'** (in this case module.modfunc()), just because if you use multiple modules then there can be many functions of same name, but if they are of same name they must be present in different files (multiple functions of same name cannot exist in a same file).

NOW, TOWARS NEXT CHAPTER:

Now, in this chapter I have discussed all the basic things about function, so just practice it by coding using function and modules and in the next chapter I will talk about **files.**

CHAPTER 9
FILES

HOW TO CREATE A FILE AND WRITE TEXTS IN IT?

Now, first I will show you an example, and then I will explain all to you.

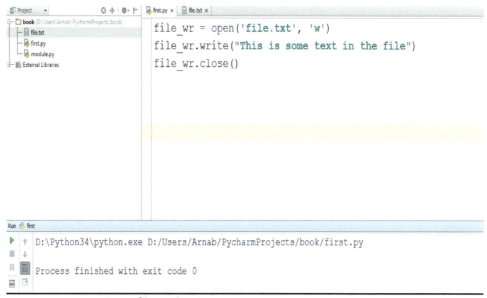

Image 9.1 – Creating a file and writing texts in it.

Explanations:

Now, here I have used an object named **'file_wr'**, you can name it whatever you want, now the keyword 'open' just opens a file, but it takes couple of parameters, first parameter is the file name (in this case 'file.txt') and next one is if you want to write or read the file, if you want to 'write' a file then use the keyword **'w'**, and if you want to read a file use the keyword **'r'**, now remember you cannot read a file without writing in it or creating it. So the first line of the code just creates file of name **'file.txt'**. And the next line is used to write contents in that file. And in the third line I have closed the file. Now remember closing a file is very much mandatory.

HOW TO READ CONTENTS FROM A FILE?

Now, I will show you how you can read text from a file, which is already created and stored in python library (When you create a python file, it is automatically stored in python library.). First look at the example then I will do the explanations.

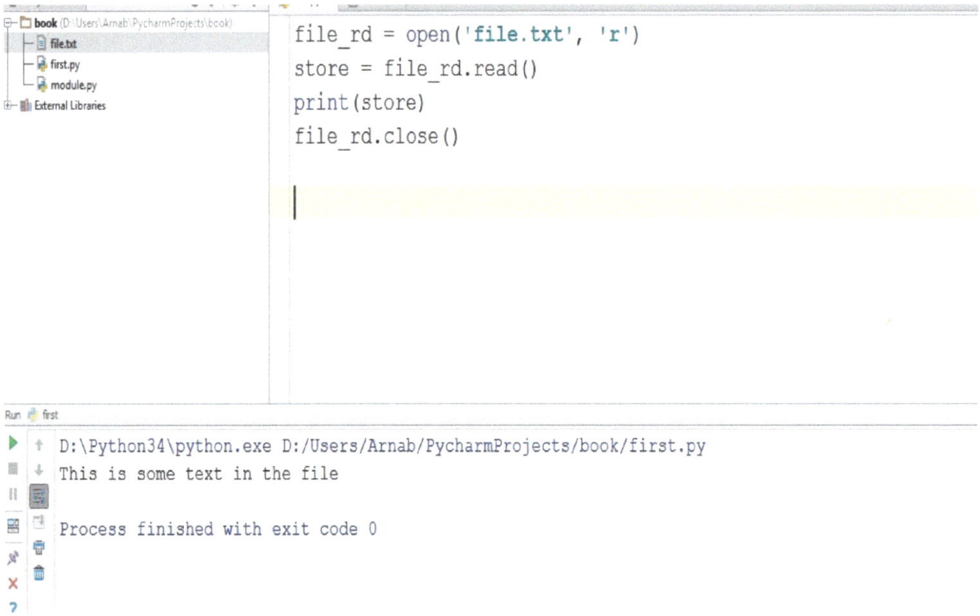

```
book (D:\Users\Arnab\PycharmProjects\book)      file_rd = open('file.txt', 'r')
    file.txt                                     store = file_rd.read()
    first.py                                     print(store)
    module.py                                    file_rd.close()
External Libraries
```

```
Run    first
    D:\Python34\python.exe D:/Users/Arnab/PycharmProjects/book/first.py
    This is some text in the file

    Process finished with exit code 0
```

Image 9.2 – Read contents from a file.

Explanations:

Now, you can see, according to image 9.2 I have used an object named **'file_rd'** ,
now again you can name your object whatever you want, now same like before
the keyword **'open'**, opens a file named 'file.txt' which is already created in
python library(during previous example.). And hence I used the keyword **'r'**.
Now I just can use what is read in the file directly, so I have to use a variable to
store the contents of file, and then I can print that content of file with the help
of that variable.

DOWNLOADING A FILE FROM INTERNET WITH PYTHON CODE:

Now, I will show you, how to download a file, with your python code, so you
don't have to use your direct downloading method form web browser to do
that, here I will download a image file using python codes.

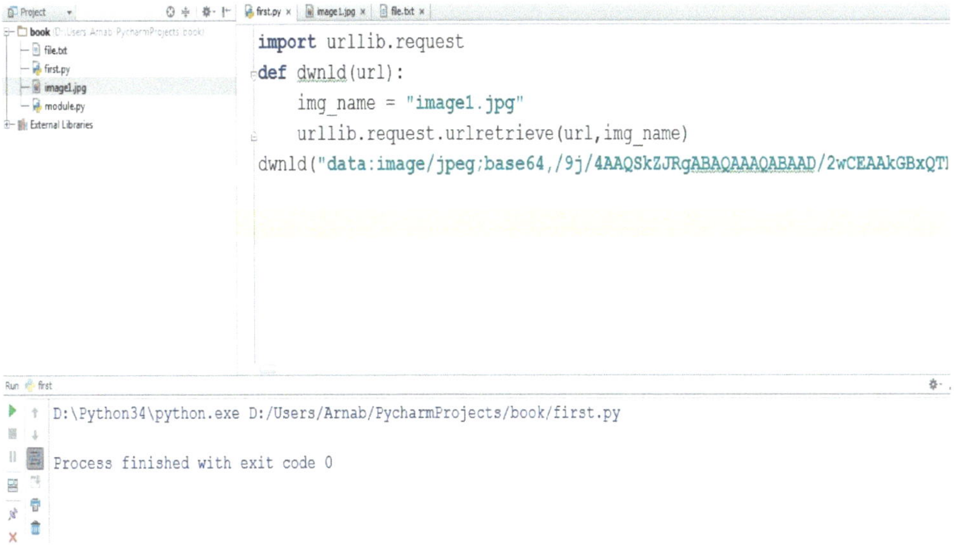

Image 9.3 – Download an image from web.

Explanations:

So, in image 9.3, you can see in the first line of code I have imported **'urllib'**, now it is a module that is already present in python3.4, and **'urllib.request'** is a function that allows to access data in a website.

Next you can see that I have created a function named **'dwnld'**, and I have passed a parameter named **'url'**, which is basically the link of that image. Next **'urllib.request.urlretrieve'** ,allows us to download image from that link, and this function takes couple of parameters, one is the link of that image and second is the name of the image by which you want to save it in your computer. And next I have passed the url in that 'dwnld' function, to complete the download, hope it is now clear to you, if it is not, you can try this kind of codes on your own and then it will be crystal clear to you. Now I am going to show you the image that I have downloaded.

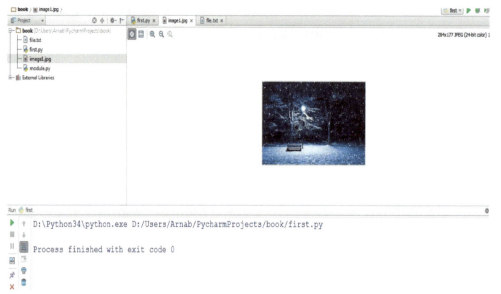

Image 9.4 – The downloaded image using python.

TIME TO MOVE ON:

So, in this chapter I have discussed about files, and I reckon more or less that is all you can get about files in python, just play around with these, practice these codes and in the next chapter I will discuss about **exception, classes and objects.**

CHAPTER 10
EXCEPTION, CLASSES AND OBJECTS

EXCEPTIONS:

WHAT IS AN EXCEPTION?

Now, I am getting straight to the point, exception is basically all about errors, but make no mistake about it, cause it is not about syntax errors, it is all about some bugs or some programming faults, (a syntax error happens due to typos, indentation errors etc.) I am telling you what is an exception? Say, you have made a program that allows the user his/her age, and you know that age is always a number, so it is of **'int'** data type, but assume that, the user has entered his/her name instead of age, so you know that name is of string data type. So when you enter your name instead of your age, the programs crashes down, and cause an exception error. I am showing you an example of an exception error.

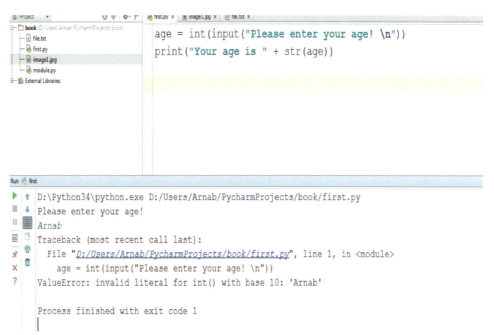

Image 10.1 – An exception error.

Explanations:

So, you can see, image 10.1 has an error, but it has no problem with its syntaxes, you can see that I have entered a string data type, where age is an integer data type, and this event forces the program to crash. And you can see that I am getting a **'Value Error'**, and it is an exception error. Let me show you how you can solve an exception error.

```python
while True:
    try:
        age = int(input("Please enter your age! \n"))
        print("Your age is " + str(age))
        break
    except ValueError:
        print("Please enter a number")
    finally:
        print("Thanks dear")
```

```
Run:    first    first
    Arnab
    Please enter a number
    Thanks dear
    Please enter your age!
    20
    Your age is 20
    Thanks dear

    Process finished with exit code 0
```

Image 10.2- Solving an exception error.

Explanations:

Now, you can see that, I have written my whole codes under a while loop, and this while loop continues the program, until it's condition is satisfied, I mean this program will continue to run until user enters a number instead of string. And, next you can see that, I have used a keyword **'try'**, and under that, I have asked used to enter his age, and it basically means just try the code which is under **'try'** block, if there are no errors just break out from the program, but if there are errors, then get out of that **'try'** block, and look for next lines of codes. Next, as you can see that I have used the keyword **'except',** and it basically means, if there is an exception error (in this case **'Value Error'**) run the codes under 'except' block. (Remember, codes under **'except'** block are not compiled, if the codes under **'try'** block are satisfied and vice versa.) And what the keyword **'finally'** is, after completing of loop each time, it just prints out a statement. So I reckon, it is now clear to your, to get more clarified view of exception errors just practice this out.

CLASSES AND OBJECTS

WHAT IS A CLASS?

Class, is a particular way of grouping several variables and functions, and this can be the simplest way you can think about class. Say, you want to make a computer game, and you want to group all of your functions, what you have made for a particular character, then you can do it using a class.

WHAT IS AN OBJECT?

Now, object is something that you need to create to get access of any variables or functions of particular class. And remember a class may have many object, all the objects under that class have the same property, and every objects that are present in a particular class are independent of each other.

Now I am trying to clarify the concept of class and object with an example.

```
class Enemy:
    life = 5
    def attack(self):
        print("enemy is attacked")
        self.life -= 1
    def check_life(self):
        print(str(self.life) + " life left")
obj1 = Enemy()
obj1.attack()
obj1.check_life()
```

```
Run:    first    first
    D:\Python34\python.exe D:/Users/Arnab/PycharmProjects/book/first.py
    enemy is attacked
    4 life left

    Process finished with exit code 0
```

Image 10.3 – Classes and objects.

Explanations:

Now, to make a class you have to use the keyword 'class', and then name it whatever you want, but I reckon it is a good practice if you name your class name with a capital letter, it helps you to differentiate between variables and functions under that class. So you can see in the example (Image 10.3) I have made a class and named it '**Enemy**', and I have used two functions and a variable under that class (Please follow the indentation order that I have made, and it is very crucial when you are dealing with classes.). Now, look very carefully, when I have declared those functions, inside the parenthesis of the functions there is a keyword '**self**', and make no mistake about it, it is not any kind of parameter that I have passed, it is just used to use any variable under that class, without the keyword '**self**', you won't be able to use the variable that is inside of that class.

Now, come to the objects, you can see there is a line of code in the program which says '**obj1 = Enemy()**', and this basically means that 'obj1' is an object of class 'Enemy', and all the properties of that class is present in that object, and without an object, it is not possible to access/use any functions or variables under a particular class. So you can see that to use the functions of that class I have used the object of that class. And the general syntax is **(object name. function name /variable name).** Hopefully it is now clear to you.

WHAT IS AN 'init' Function?

Now, **'init'** is a special type of **predefined** function which is used in python, whenever you create an object inside a class this function gets called automatically, I mean you don't have to call this function exclusively to use it. I know, it may sound little bit weird, but I am showing you an example and it should make the things clear to you.

```
class Friends:
    def __init__(self):
        self.st1 = str(input("Enter your favourite game!\n"))
        print("You love " + self.st1)
obj1 = Friends()
```

```
D:\Python34\python.exe D:/Users/Arnab/PycharmProjects/book/first.py
Enter your favourite game!
Medal Of Honor
You love Medal Of Honor

Process finished with exit code 0
```

Image 10.4 An init function.

Explanations:
Now, the very first thing I need to mention is when you are using an 'init' function use two underscore signs before the keyword **'init'** and two underscore signs after the keyword **'init'** (like this __init__). Now you can see that I have made a simple program inside that 'init' class which allows you to enter a name, and when I used this class, I didn't take any help of any object, I just made an object of that class, and the function is called automatically. This is why 'init' function is different than all other functions. Now you probably thinking what is the advantages of it, as this functions gives you kind of lesser controls on the program. Well, I will discuss more about this function and show you why it is useful, in GUI (Graphical User interfacing) part of this book, and then it will be easier for you to understand.

TOWARDS NEXT CHAPTER:

So, this is all the basics about an exception errors , classes and object, hopefully most of the things are clear to you, and to get a detailed view practice these codes on your own, I reckon it will help you a lot. And in the next chapter I will talk about **inheritance and threading.**

CHAPTER 11
INHERITACE AND THREADING

What is inheritance?

In simple words inheritance is getting something from others, what you don't have, let me give you a practical example, say your eyes are same as your father's, that means that you have inherited that property from your father, similarly if your mom gives you $100, that means you have inherited that money from your mom. Now, similarly in computer programming the properties of any class can be inherited to another class, let me show you a simple example of that.

```python
class Parent():
    def eyes_color(self):
        self.color = 'Blue'
        print("My eye color is  " + self.color)
class Child(Parent):
    def name(self):
        print("My name is Arnab Banerjee ")
obj1 = Child()
obj1.eyes_color()
obj1.name()
```

```
D:\Python34\python.exe D:/Users/Arnab/PycharmProjects/book/first.py
My eye color is  Blue
My name is Arnab Banerjee

Process finished with exit code 0
```

Image 11.1- A simple inheritance.

Explanations:

Now you can see in the example (in image 11.1), there are two classes one is parent class another one is child class, but you can name your class whatever you want. Now you can see under that parent class I have made a function, and under child class also there is a function, but you can see when I made the child class, in between the parenthesis, I have passed parent class, and that's how you can inherit properties from one class to another class. Now you can see that I have made an object **'obj1'** for the child class, but whenever I want to access the **'eyes_color'** function with that object I can do it successfully, though that function was under parent class. So I can do it just because, all the properties of that parent class is inherited into the child class. And like one class to another, inheritance also can be possible from multiple classes to one class and one class to multiple classes, but the syntax is basically same. So this is all the basic about inheritance.

WHAT IS THREADING?

Say, if you have two processes in your computer and you want to run them at the same time simultaneously with your python code, then concept of threading comes into play. Let me show you an example.

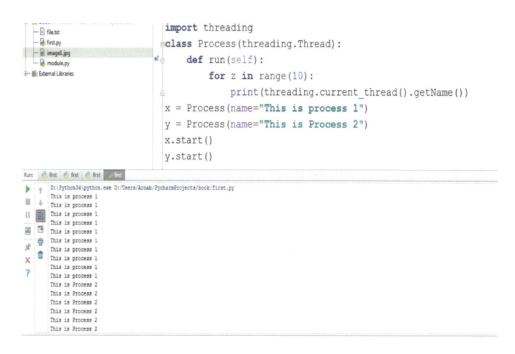

```python
import threading
class Process(threading.Thread):
    def run(self):
        for z in range(10):
            print(threading.current_thread().getName())
x = Process(name="This is process 1")
y = Process(name="This is Process 2")
x.start()
y.start()
```

```
Run:   first    first    first    first
  ▶  ↑   D:\Python34\python.exe D:/Users/Arnab/PycharmProjects/book/first.py
         This is process 1
  ■  ↓   This is process 1
  ‖      This is process 1
         This is process 1
  ≛  ☐   This is process 1
         This is process 1
  ⚹  ☐   This is process 1
  ✕      This is process 1
  ?      This is process 1
         This is process 1
         This is Process 2
         This is Process 2
         This is Process 2
         This is Process 2
         This is Process 2
         This is Process 2
```

Image 11.2 – Threading.

Explanations:

I will do a line by line explanations for the given example(In image 11.2) and I reckon it will help you to understand about it more easily, so let's start. Now in the first line of the code you can see that I have imported **'threading'**, and this is mandatory when you want to thread a program, in the second line I have made a class named **'Process'**, and you can see that I have passed **'threading. Thread'** in that **'Process'** class, that means **'threading'** is a parent class, and I have inherited that property in the class that I have made now, so if I don't import **'threading'**, actually I won't be able to use that as a parent class, in the class that I have made now, now in the third line I have made a function called **'run'**, now remember it is a built in function, whenever you are working with threading, you have to name your function **'run'**, otherwise it will cause some errors. And in next couple of lines what I wanted to do is, I wanted to make two different threads with two different names and I wanted to print out their names for 10 times. So, you can see in the 6th and 7th line I have created two different threads, with two different names, **'x'** and **'y'**. And remember when you want to run your threads the syntax is **'thread name. start'**, so in this case I have written **'x. start'** and **'y. start'** to run the **'x'** and **'y'** threads. And remember whenever you use the 'start' function, it just go into the class and look for the 'run' function, and then it compiles the codes under the **'run'** function, Hence it is mandatory to name your function 'run' whenever you are dealing with threading.

TIME TO LEARN SOME GUIs:

So, this is all the basics about inheritance and threading, hopefully now you know what these things are. Just practice these things out more and more to get habituated and in our next and last chapter we will talk about some interesting staffs and that is **GUIs. (Graphical User Interfacing.)**

CHAPTER 12
GUIs or GRAPHICAL USER INTERFACING

WHAT IS GUI?

GUI, is basically an interface programing, that uses the computer graphics facility, and allows the user to interact with the program graphically, a simple example of a GUI is a basic window with a minimize, maximize and cross button in it, and some buttons, labels, drop down menus can be added as well, I will show how you can make some simple GUIs. And I will start from very basic.

CREATE A BASIC WINDOW:

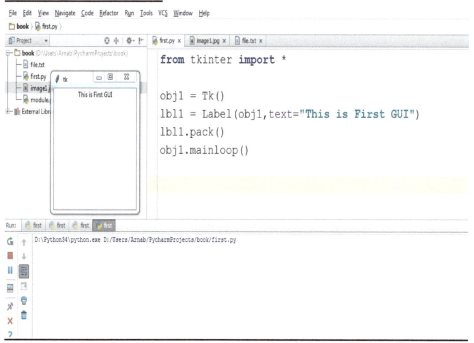

Image 12.1 – A basic window.

Explanations:

Now, you can see that in the example(image 12.1) I have created a basic window with python code, so it is time for little bit explanations of that code, now before I start, you need to know about one more thing and that is **'tkinter'**, it is basically a built in library that comes with core python and you need to use it when you are dealing with GUI, cause all the GUI classes of python are stored into this library, so in the first line you can see that I have written **'from tkinter import * '** and this basically means import all the classes from **'tkinter'** library. And in the next line I have created an object **'obj1'** for **'Tk()'** class, and this is also a built in class, which is needed for creating a basic window, and in the next line I have created a variable **'lbl1'** to store a Label (**A Label is basically about writing any text in your window**), and it takes couple of parameters, first is the place where you want to have your label, well of course when you are making a basic window, you want to have your label in that window, hence I have used the object of **'Tk()'** class and the second parameter is what text you want to have as your label. So when you have created these staffs, you want to display those staffs on the window you have made, and that's what the code 'lbl1. pack ' means, it means basically pack those staffs on your window to display. And the last line of the program **'obj1. mainloop()'** is very much essential, cause whenever you create a window you need it to stay it on the screen until you close it manually, so, when you create a window without this code, since is computer is very fast your window just pops up and closes automatically in a blink of an eye, so to make your window stay on the screen you need the program to run continuously, and that's what that line of code does, it basically runs the code in main loop and never stops, until the user closes the window manually.

CREATING FRAMES AND BUTTONS:
First look at the code how to do it and then I will explain how it is working.

```python
from tkinter import *
obj1 = Tk()
frm1 = Frame(obj1)
frm1.pack(side = TOP)
frm2 = Frame(obj1)
frm2.pack(side = BOTTOM)
but1 = Button(frm1, text ="click me", fg = "Blue", bg = "Green")
but1.pack()
but2 = Button(frm2, text = "Second button", fg ="Yellow", bg = "Red")
but2.pack()
obj1.mainloop()
```

Image 12.2 – Creating frames and buttons.

Explanations:
Now, from the last explanations you know what the first two lines and the last line of this program does, so, I am starting from the 3rd line where you can see that I have made a variable **'frm1'**, to create a frame(**A frame can basically separate tor window into some parts, with invisible lines**), now since I want to

have my frame on the window that I have made, I have passed object of **'Tk()'** class, then I have packed that frame and since I wanted to have that frame on the top side of my window I have passed a parameter **'side = TOP'**, and similarly I made another frame and packed it in the bottom side of my window. Then I have created couple of buttons with the help of variables **'but1'** and **'but2'**, and it takes few parameters, since I wanted to have my first button on the top frame of my window (**'frm1'**)I have passed that value, and the second parameter is what You want to display as text on your button, for the first button I named it **'Click me'** as you can see in the example, and the last parameter **'fg'** basically sets the color of the fonts in the button, and if you want to have a background color of your button you can pass another variable **'bg'** and then set it equal to the color name. Then similarly like the first button I have created another button and placed it in the bottom frame of the window, and you can spot the difference between the positions of the buttons in that window when it is displayed, so hopefully things are bit clear to you, but to understand these things clearly you have to practice these things out.

THE GRID LAYOUT:

Grid layout is more advanced layout than **'pack'**, and it gives the programmer more control as well as it allows to deal with rows and columns of a layout. Let me show you an example.

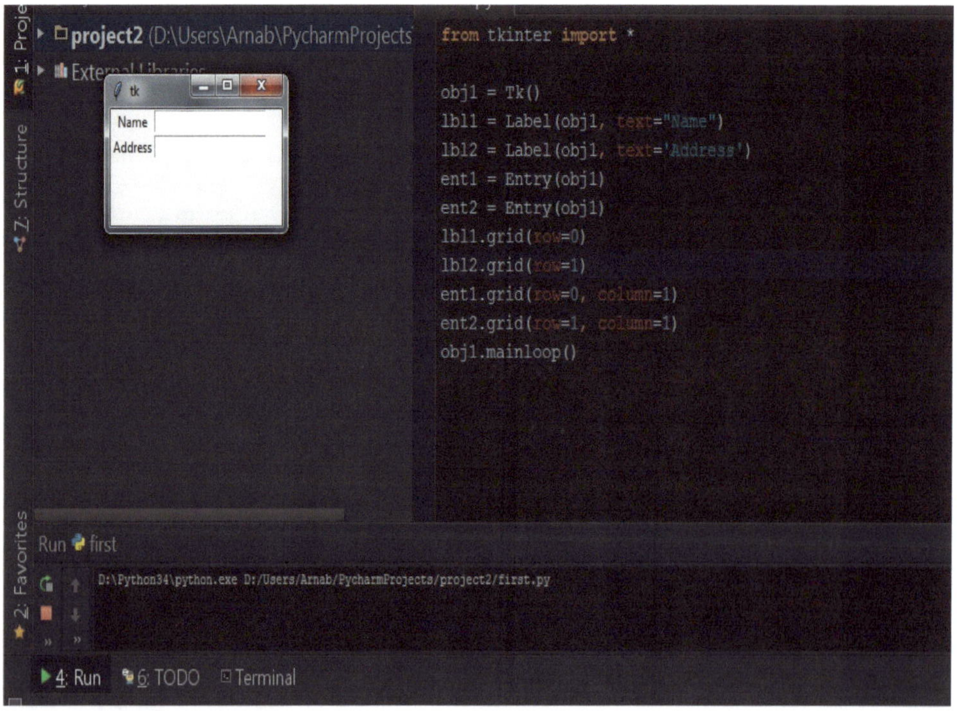

Image 12.3- Grid layout.

So far, we have used 'pack' function when we were dealing with GUIs, but now I will talk about a new layout and it is called 'grid', and why you want to know about it? Just because it because more controls over the other layouts, say if you want to arrange some buttons row and column wise in your window, so to do that you have to use 'grid' layout, you can't do it with a plain 'pack' layout. So you can see in this example I have arranged the widgets row and column wise, and here I have used a new widget also, which is called 'Entry' (this is kind of a blank text field). You can see I have used two variables 'lbl1' and 'lbl2' to create two labels and other two variables 'ent1' and 'ent2' to create couple of 'Entries' or blank text field. Now since computer starts counting from zero if you want to place your widget at first row make sure that your row =0 and if you want to place it at second row make row = 1 , same rule also applicable for columns as well. Now if you look at the code and the GUI that it has made carefully you will surely understand the rest of the codes.

ADDING FUNCTIONALITY TO THE WIDGETS:

Now, so far we have made some windows, buttons, text fields etc. but they were just a still screen, they were not functioning, I mean if you click one button, nothing will happen, so it is time for add little bit functionality to those widgets. So that they can work a bit, I am showing you a demonstration first and then I will explain what I have done to add those functionalities.

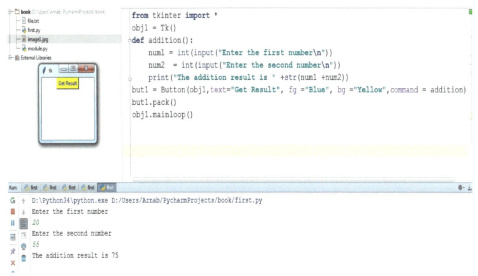

Image 12.4 – Adding functionality to the widgets.

Explanations:

So, include bit of functioning in our GUI, I have made a function(as you can see in image 12.4) that does a simple addition program, and prints out the result, after that you can see that I have created a button, and as you know it takes few parameters as I have discussed about it earlier, but here I have passed another new parameter which is called **'command'**, (**this parameter basically adds the function to your button, and functionality to your GUI**.) and set it equal to the function, which I want to add on my button, and remember don't use parenthesis after your function name, just use the name of your function and that's all, this function does not need any parameter to pass. So after my GUI is created, when I hit the button you can see my function is executed on the command lines. So this should be very easy to you, just play around with this, add more functionalities at your will, and make sure you have done all the syntax rightly.

SUMMARY:

So, now you know, how to create basic GUIs with python, now you know how a function can work in a button, so this should give a basic idea how python works on GUIs, but GUI is not limited in these things, it can be more advanced, but since this book is for beginners, I am not showing you the advanced GUIs, just because it will require more advanced knowledge, but if you go through this book thoroughly you can launch yourself to more advanced python programming and can think about it as well.

So, that is all I had to share in this book, hopefully it will come in your benefits.